# IMAGES
# OF
# CHRIST

*A Celebration*

# IMAGES OF CHRIST
*A Celebration*

CROSSROAD . NEW YORK

# THE ADORATION

~

As in many of the traditional paintings of the Nativity of Christ, the light in this picture is not only focused on the Christ child, but also radiates out from the Light of the World, casting beams of divine light on the blessed Virgin Mary and the worshipping shepherds. The atmosphere of an animal's stable is the strong secondary theme here, with the manger, the straw, the cattle, and even two chickens emphazising the humble birth of the King of Kings.

> *And there were shepherds living out in the fields near by, keeping watch over their flocks at night. And an angel of the Lord appeared to them ... and said to them ... "Do not be afraid. I bring you good news of great joy that will be for all the people. Today in the town of David a Saviour has been born to you; he is Christ the Lord." ... So they hurried off and found Mary and Joseph, and the baby, who was lying in a manger.*
>
> LUKE 2:8–11,16

THE ADORATION OF THE SHEPHERDS
*Bartolome Esteban Murillo, 1618–1682*

# The Flight into Egypt

The holy family has to flee from Bethlehem to escape the edge of King Herod's sword, as all the male children up to two years of age are slaughtered. The flight into Egypt is a favorite scene among traditional religious artists. Mary, draped in blue, the color of heaven, has the Christ child safely in her arms. Joseph, painted as an old man, is thought to have died of old age before Jesus was thirty.

> *An angel of the Lord appeared to Joseph in a dream. "Get up," he said, "take the child and his mother and escape to Egypt. Stay there until I tell you, for Herod is going to search for the child to kill him."*
>
> *So he got up, took the child and his mother during the night and left for Egypt, where he stayed until the death of Herod.*
>
> MATTHEW 2:13–15

Vespers, The Flight into Egypt
*Playfair Book of Hours, late 15th century*

# Nazareth

The holy family had traveled from Nazareth up to Jerusalem for the annual Passover celebration with their friends and neighbors, but, as they return home, they are alone. The twelve-year-old Christ had delayed in the temple talking with the religious leaders. Dobson's painting clearly depicts the ages of the three figures. Mary, a teenager when Jesus was born, is now in her twenties. Christ, a twelve-year-old, is not yet strong enough to walk the whole journey home. Joseph's face and walk show him to be many years Mary's senior.

> *Every year his parents went to Jerusalem for the Feast of the Passover. When Jesus was twelve years old, they went up to the Feast, as was their custom... After three days they found Jesus in the temple courts, sitting among the teachers, listening to them and asking them questions ...Then Jesus went down to Nazareth with Mary and Joseph and was obedient to them.*
>
> LUKE 2:41–2,46,51

JESUS RETURNING TO NAZARETH
WITH HIS PARENTS
*William Charles Thomas Dobson, 1817–1898*

# JOSEPH

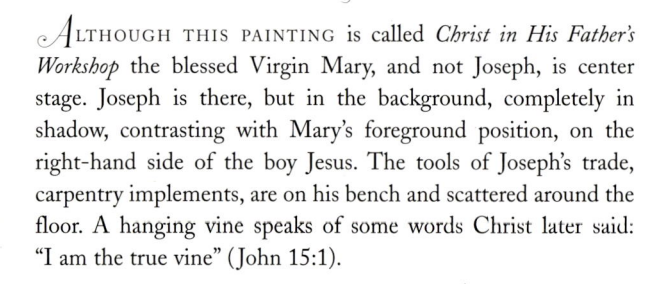

Although this painting is called *Christ in His Father's Workshop* the blessed Virgin Mary, and not Joseph, is center stage. Joseph is there, but in the background, completely in shadow, contrasting with Mary's foreground position, on the right-hand side of the boy Jesus. The tools of Joseph's trade, carpentry implements, are on his bench and scattered around the floor. A hanging vine speaks of some words Christ later said: "I am the true vine" (John 15:1).

> *Joseph and Mary ... returned to Galilee to their own town of Nazareth. And the child grew and became strong; he was filled with wisdom, and the grace of God was upon him.*
>
> LUKE 2:39–40

CHRIST IN HIS
FATHER'S WORKSHOP
*Jean-Baptiste Auguste Lelor,
1809–1870*

# Baptism

$\backsim$

$\mathcal{C}$HRIST, IS BEING baptized by John The Baptist in the River Jordan. Some Christian denominations, such as the Baptists, still take the scene depicted in this painting as a precedent to baptize people by fully immersing them in water, rather than just making the sign of the cross on their foreheads with water. God's Spirit, in the form of a dove, is seen descending on Christ.

> *Jesus came from Galilee to the Jordan to be baptized by John. As soon as Jesus was baptized, he went up out of the water. At that moment the heaven was opened, and he saw the Spirit of God descending like a dove and lighting on him. And a voice from heaven said, "This is my Son, whom I love; with him I am well pleased."*
>
> MATTHEW 3:13, 16–17

THE BAPTISM OF CHRIST
*Soane Book of Hours, c.1500*

# LAZARUS

*C*HRIST, WITH HIS ARM RAISED and his disciples behind him, visits the grave of his close friend, Lazarus, who has been dead for four days. Lazarus' sisters, Mary and Martha, kneel before Christ. In the picture, Christ has just ordered the stone to be rolled away from the cave-grave, and has called out, "Lazarus, come out!" Lazarus, still wrapped in his grave clothes, emerges, to everyone's astonishment. In the center is a group of Jews, some of whom, then, believed in Christ, while others ran off to complain to the Pharisees.

> *"Where have you laid him?" Jesus asked.*
> *"Come and see, Lord," they replied.*
> *Jesus wept.*
> *Jesus, once more deeply moved, came to the tomb …They took away the stone … Jesus called out in a loud voice, "Lazarus, come out!" The dead man came out, his hands and feet wrapped with strips of linen, and a cloth around his face.*
>
> JOHN 11:34,35,38,41,43,44

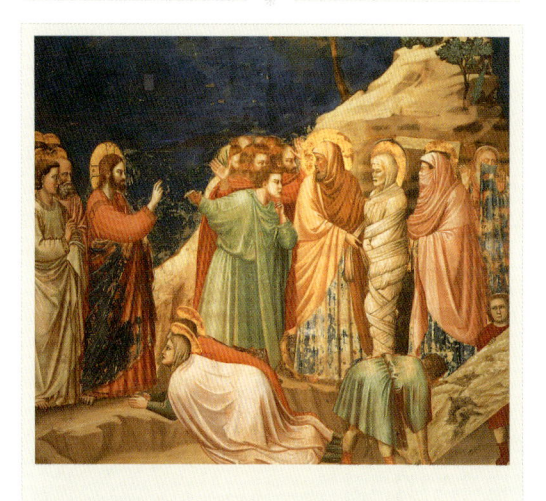

THE RESURRECTION OF LAZARUS
*Giotto di Bondone, 1276–1337*

# JESUS IN THE TEMPLE

$C$HRIST IS in the center of this picture, traditionally known as the "Cleansing of the temple," and it is just possible to see a whip in his hand. The scene shows the sheep, cattle, and a caged bird, all about to be sold as temple sacrifices. Christ, in anger, overturns the money changers' tables, and is about to use his whip to drive out these traders from the temple's courtyard. Behind the money changers, the Pharisees plot Jesus' downfall, while, on the other side, Jesus' disciples watch in amazement.

> *In the temple courts Jesus found men selling cattle, sheep and doves, and others sitting at tables exchanging money. So he made a whip out of cords, and drove all from the temple area, both sheep and cattle, he scattered the coins of the money changers and overturned their tables. To those who sold doves he said, "Get these out of here! How dare your turn my Father's house into a market!"*
>
> JOHN 2:14–16

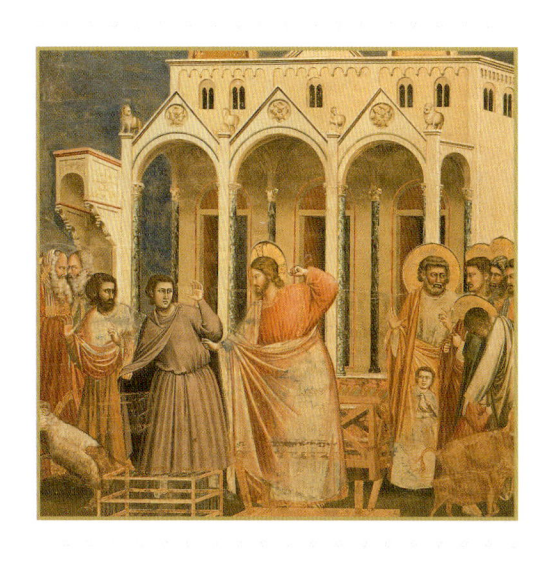

JESUS EXPELS IDOLATORS FROM THE TEMPLE
*Giotto di Bondone, 1276–1337*

# WASHING PETER'S FEET

*One of the most* menial tasks a slave performed for his master was to wash his feet, as sandals gave no protection from the hot, dusty streets. Christ has removed his outer clothing, put a towel round his waist, and washes Peter's feet, just as a slave would. The other disciples recline at the table where the Lord's Supper will shortly be instituted. Headstrong Peter, after his initial protest to Christ, now bows his head in thought as his Master washes his feet.

> *Jesus got up from the meal, took off his outer clothing, and wrapped a towel round his waist. After that, he poured water into a basin and began to wash his disciples' feet, drying them with the towel that was wrapped round him. He came to Simon Peter, who said to him, "Lord, you are going to wash my feet?"*
>
> *Jesus replied, "You do not realize now what I am doing, but later you will understand."*
>
> *"No," said Peter, "you shall never wash my feet."*
>
> *Jesus answered, "Unless I wash you, you have not part of me."*
>
> *"Then, Lord," Simon Peter replied, "not just my feet but my hands and my head as well."*
>
> JOHN 13:4–9

JESUS WASHING PETER'S FEET
*Ford Maddox Brown, 1821–1893*

# THE SUFFERING CHRIST

Artists have struggled to depict the suffering Christ. Here Morales emphazises both Christ as a human being, and Christ as divine. The crown of thorns has real, sharp thorns, producing real crimson, flowing blood. It matches the scarlet robe which the soldiers had put on Christ, along with the staff in his right hand, as they made fun of him. The light surrounding the crown of thorns points to Christ's divinity.

> *The soldiers stripped Christ and put a scarlet robe on him, and then twisted together a crown of thorns and set it on his head. They put a staff in his right hand and knelt in front of him and mocked him. "Hail, king of the Jews!" they said. They spat on him, and took the staff and struck him on the head again and again.*
>
> MATTHEW 27:28–30

ECCE HOMO
*Luis Morales, 1509–1586*

# They Crucified Jesus

*Hans Memlinc's* depiction of the crucifixion of Christ is highly stylized and firmly set in the fifteenth century, with its castle in the background, and horses and soldiers of that period. However, there are numerous details which faithfully reflect the gospels' account of Jesus' death. He is crucified between two other men, he has a notice giving the charge against him above his head, and his side is pierced by a soldier. On the ground, the bones indicate that it was a place of public persecution, and nearly all those concerned about Jesus are women. Above, the sky is dark.

> *At noon the whole country was covered with darkness, which lasted for three hours. One of the soldiers pierced Jesus' side with a spear, bringing a sudden flow of blood and water.*
>
> John 19:34

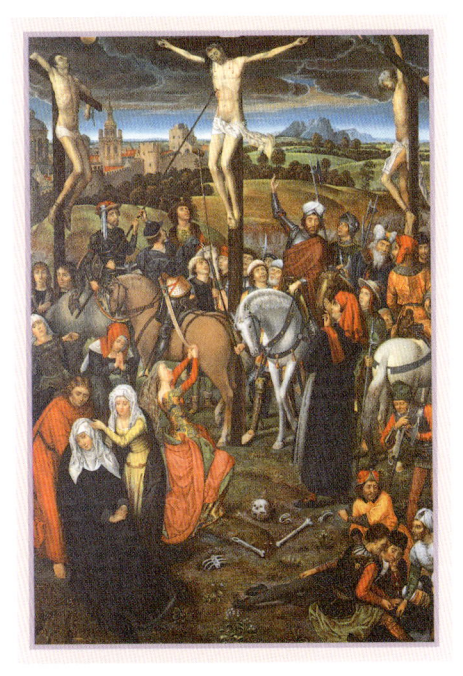

THE CRUCIFIXION
*Hans Memlinc, late 15th century*

# Light of the World

*D*EATH HAUNTED the ancient world. The stench of death pervades Paton's painting. Scattered skeletons litter the ground, while the whole scene is shrouded in thick darkness. Christ gently takes the hand of humanity in her hopelessness. He brings hope to the valley of the shadow of death in several ways. The light around Christ's head speaks of him being the Light of the World, his crown of thorns and his nail-pierced hand speak of his identification with suffering, while the cross he carries points to heaven.

> *Even though I walk*
> *through the valley of the shadow of death,*
> *I will fear no evil,*
> *for you are with me;*
> *your rod and your staff,*
> *they comfort me.*
>
> PSALM 23:4

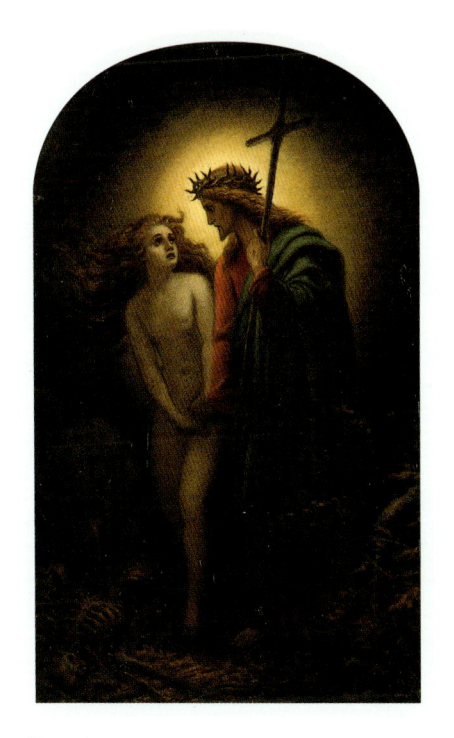

THE VALLEY OF THE SHADOW OF DEATH
*Joseph Noel Paton, 1822–1901*

# SEA OF GALILEE

*At first glance* this beautiful scene of the Sea of Galilee could be at any time in Jesus' ministry, with some of his fishermen disciples in their boat. But from the title of the painting we are told that it must be St. Peter in the water, wading ashore to land. The significant detail in the painting is the two fish cooking over the fire. This event is recorded by St. John as one of the times when Christ showed himself to be alive to his disciples, after his crucifixion.

> *Then the disciple whom Jesus loved said to Peter, "It is the Lord!" As soon as Simon Peter heard him say, "It is the Lord," he ... jumped into the water. The other disciples followed in the boat ... When they landed, they saw a fire of burning coals with fish on it ... This was now the third time Jesus appeared to his disciples after he was raised from the dead.*
>
> JOHN 21:7,9,14

CHRIST, ST. PETER AND THE DISCIPLES
ON THE SEA OF GALILEE
*Lucas Gassel*

# The Resurrection

The influence of the Italian master painter, Raphael, and his works of grandeur are not hard to detect in this painting by the Frenchman Eustache Le Sueur. Christ descends from the clouds. His followers raise their heads, train their eyes on him, and open their arms in welcome. The two foreground figures, the angelic-like "harpist" and the woman reclining, eating delectable fruit, set the atmosphere of praise and delight at the coming presence of the divine Master.

> *Christ ... was raised on the third day according to the Scriptures, and ... appeared to Peter, and then to the Twelve. After that, he appeared to more than five hundred of the brothers at the same time, most of whom are still living ... Then he appeared to James, then to all the apostles, and last of all he appeared to me.*
>
> 1 Corinthians 15:3–7

The Risen Christ
Approaching the Disciples
*Eustache Le Sueur, c.1617–1655*

# STIGMATA

$\mathcal{B}$ELLINI, whom Albrecht Dürer called the most important Venetian painter of his day, captures Christ's assumption, as he rises from earth into the clouds and sky of heaven, in a most striking fashion. The risen Christ still bears the stigmata of the nails, the crown of thorns and the wound in his side. He carries the Book of Life, with the names of the redeemed inscribed in it. His hand is raised as he blesses his followers and the whole world.

> *The soldiers crucified Jesus ... One of the soldiers pierced Jesus' side with a spear, bringing a sudden flow of blood and water.*
>
> JOHN 19:23,34

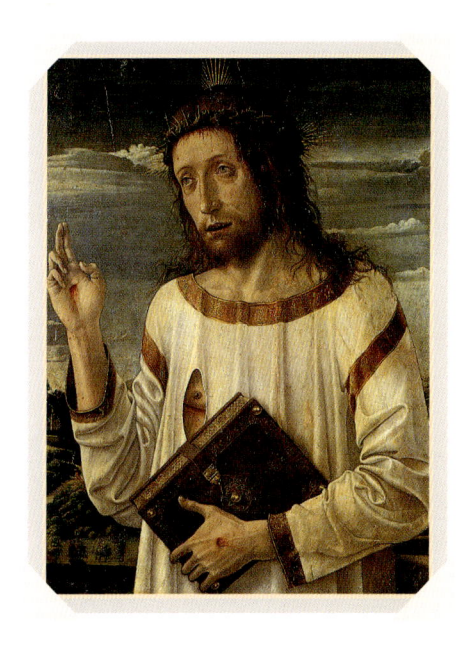

CHRIST BLESSING, SHOWING STIGMATA
AND CARRYING BOOK
*Giovanni Bellini, 1429–1516*

Copyright © 1996 by HUNT & THORPE

Text © 1996 by *Mark Water*

THE CROSSROAD PUBLISHING COMPANY
370 Lexington Avenue, New York, NY 10017

Designed by THE BRIDGEWATER BOOK COMPANY LIMITED

All rights reserved. No part of this book may be reproduced,
stored in a retrieval system, or transmitted, in any form or
by any means, electronic, mechanical, photocopying,
recording, or otherwise, without prior written
permission from the publisher
THE CROSSROAD PUBLISHING COMPANY.

Printed and bound in Singapore.

ISBN 0-8245-1570-6

The publishers wish to thank the following for the use of pictures:
E.T. ARCHIVE: Louvre, Paris p. 31; Prado, Madrid p.5; Scrovegni Chapel,
Padua pp.15,17; Sir John Soane's Museum, London p.13;
Tate Gallery p.19; Victoria & Albert Museum p.7;
FINE ART PHOTOGRAPHIC: cover, title page, pp.9,11,
half title page and 21,23,25,27,29.

*Cover illustration*
*Entry of Christ into Jerusalem*, Luca Giordano